THIS IS
SCOTLAND

DESIGNED AND EDITED
BY
JENNY CARTER

FONTANA/COLLINS
London and Glasgow

First Published by
FONTANA/COLLINS 1981
London, Glasgow, Sydney, Auckland, Toronto, Johannesburg

This book was designed and edited by Jenny Carter
Production by Stephen King and Ken Smith

Paperback ISBN 0 00 636423 3
Hardback ISBN 0 00 435670 5

Photographs © Photo Precision Ltd., St. Ives, Huntingdon
Text © Fontana 1981

Origination and Printing: Photo Precision Ltd, St. Ives, Huntingdon
Binding: Oxford University Press, Oxford

CONTENTS

Scotland

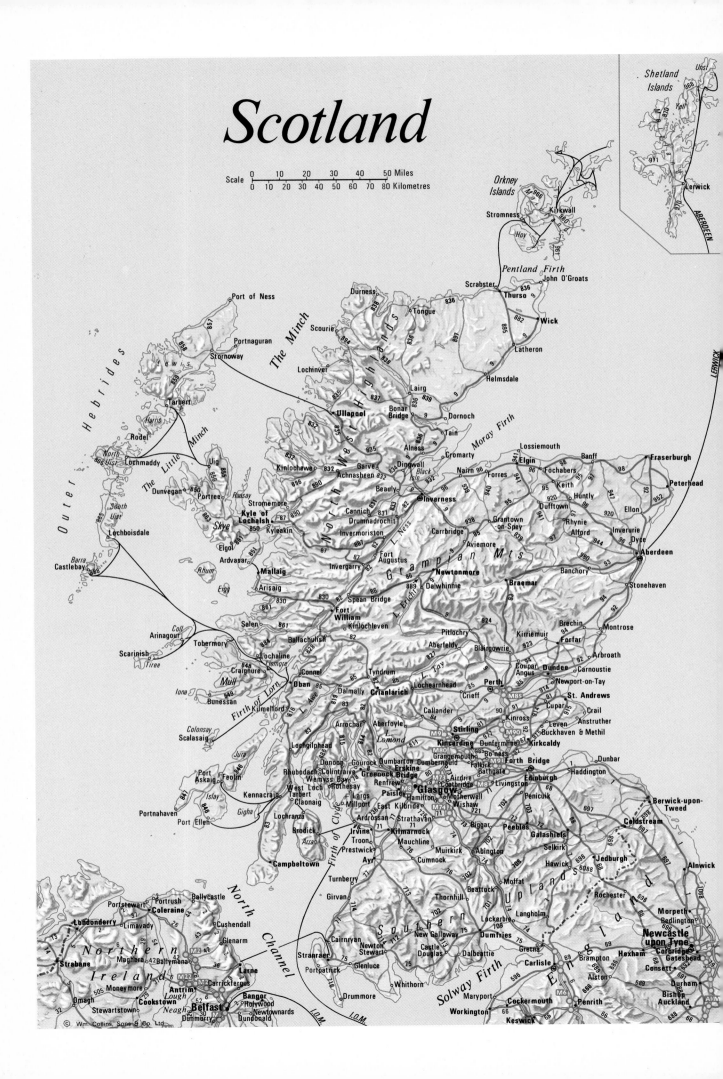

Introduction

There is no one Scotland: and no single image that can stand for this country of infinite variety. From Border homestead to simple island croft via the elegant dwellings of Edinburgh is a long journey in more than miles. Between lies a nation—that of the Scots.

Visitors to Scotland will treasure their own images of this beautiful country. Many will explore its capital, Edinburgh, that nonpareil of cities with its unrivalled thoroughfare, Princes Street, undoubtedly one of the finest streets in the world; many will come here for the Festival in the autumn—the biggest arts festival in the world—or will wind their way up the Royal Mile to the Castle esplanade to witness the spectacle of the Military Tattoo or simply to admire the splendid views.

Glasgow, showpiece of Victorian expansion, opens the routes to the ports of the Clyde, where the natives no less than foreigners enjoy the sailing and the beaches, and get away from it all 'doon the water'. South is Ayrshire—'Burns Country'—where annually pilgrims make their way to the homelands of the Bard.

The Border Abbeys stand serene and silent now, witness to centuries of Christian worship; and around them life in the Border towns centres still on the age-old occupations of farming and weaving, while the enthusiastic shouts of rugby supporters break the sharp air on a winter Saturday. Castles are here in plenty; for here, near the old enemy England, there was always a need for defence. Now many stand ruined; union with the south at length brought peace.

The history of this fascinating land is everywhere in evidence. Stirling Castle stands proud on its rocky knoll looking out over five great battlefields at this key strategic site. Across the flat lands of the carse, the rugged Wallace Monument pays tribute to William Wallace, the great fighter for Scottish independence, and at nearby Bannockburn Robert Bruce, champion of that cause, is immortalised in statue.

Across the Forth from Edinburgh lies Fife, the 'royal kingdom', with its ancient Falkland Palace, and the splendid abbey at Dunfermline, burial place of kings. Fishing is Fife's trade, and the picturesque coastal villages look ever to the harbour and the nets.

Inland and further north, the country grows more mountainous, and the hills and lochs give us the land of purple majesty where deer roam free and the whir of the wings of grouse hangs sweet on the air in autumn. Here the walker may stretch his legs and his eyes too, and find his place in all this vastness of land and sky. In the north the living is off the land, and crofts huddle into villages, or straggle out over the peaty moors.

Towns are few in this rugged terrain: Inverness oversees the key routes in the north, Oban is the focus of the west, and Aberdeen, undoubtedly one of the fastest developing cities in all Britain, commands the plains of the north east. Offshore, not just trawlers but oil supply vessels ply to and fro, servicing the oil rigs in the North Sea bonanza.

Scattered round the coast, in the north and west, are Scotland's islands—some six hundred of them; and they are almost little nations in themselves, for each has a character all its own. Orkney, Shetland, Fair Isle, the 'Long Isle', Skye, Mull, Islay—it takes a persistent visitor to become acquainted with them all.

No camera can capture the smell of the air, no book compress the vastness of these open spaces. But look through these pages; and we hope you will find something of the Scotland you enjoyed, and perhaps something new to delight.

Opposite The River Tweed

The South East

The area of the Borders around Jedburgh and Melrose is called 'Scott Country', so strong are its associations with this great Scottish novelist and poet. **Above**, a view of the Eildon hills, much loved by Sir Walter Scott; and **left**, the writer's home, Abbotsford, purchased by him in 1812.

Queen Mary's House, Jedburgh (**opposite**), where the Queen is said to have lain ill after riding to nearby Hermitage Castle to meet her lover Bothwell in 1566.

Above, Melrose Abbey, one of the great Border Abbeys founded in a period of great religious fervour in the 12th century. The heart of King Robert Bruce is supposed to be buried here. **Left**, Dryburgh Abbey, where Sir Walter Scott is buried. All the Border Abbeys were attacked many times by the English, and only ruins now remain.

The Borders, so near the enemy England, were very vulnerable to attack, and to provide protection strong castles were built, such as Neidpath, near Peebles (**below**), which dates back to the 13th century, and has walls eleven feet thick.

By contrast, Floors Castle at Kelso, **right**, seat of the Duke of Roxburghe, is superbly elegant. Built after the Union, in an age of increasing peacefulness, the need for defence had gone. Floors lies in splendid parkland, with fine views of nearby Kelso, and the distant Cheviots.

Left, Eyemouth was once a notorious smuggling centre, for caves abound along this rocky coastline; it is still an active port, where trawlers regularly land their catches.

Above St Abbs lies to the north of Eyemouth, a tiny village at the foot of impressive cliffs. Nearby is St Abb's Head, renowned for its spectacular scenery and towering cliffs with their colonies of nesting seabirds.

Dunbar, mid-way between Edinburgh and the English border, suffered many attacks. In 1338 the castle, **right**, was defended by 'Black Agnes', who is said to have dusted the battlements with her handkerchief as a sign of contempt for her attackers.

Below, top Tantallon Castle is built on a rocky promontory, defended on the seaward side only by the cliffs. From the towering walls, the views across the Forth to the Bass Rock are excellent. On the rock, gannets nest in their thousands.

Below, foot Preston Mill near East Linton is still in perfect working order, even though parts of the building date back to the 17th century.

Edinburgh, Scotland's capital city, is dominated by the proud outline of the Castle, perched high on its rock; the views from the battlements (**below, top**) are superb. For centuries this was the guardian of the city, focus at first for the little garrison town, later a royal residence before the Palace of Holyroodhouse was developed and took over that role.

Princes Street is the city's main thoroughfare, and one of the finest streets in Europe. On one side are the shops, the other lies open to the attractive Princes Street Gardens, lying below the cliffs of the castle. Here is found the Scott Monument, **right**, the nation's tribute to Sir Walter Scott.

Above Edinburgh Castle from Princes Street Gardens.

Centre The Palace of Holyroodhouse, Edinburgh residence of Her Majesty the Queen. Holyrood lies at the foot of the 'Royal Mile', which runs from the Castle to the gates of the Palace; behind lie the glorious open spaces of the Queen's Park, with its distinctive outcrops, Arthur's Seat and the Salisbury Crags.

Left John Knox's House lies about half way down the Royal Mile; here the fiery Reformation preacher is said to have lived.

Above Every autumn during the Edinburgh International Festival, a Military Tattoo is held on the Castle Esplanade.

Right, 'Greyfriars's Bobby', a little dog who faithfully kept watch by his master's grave for many years, is commemorated by this statue outside Greyfriar's Kirk.

Right The old buildings of Dean Village, now very much a part of Edinburgh, but at one time a village well outside the city boundaries.

Below A burst of springtime glory in Edinburgh's Royal Botanic Gardens.

The Forth Bridges link
Edinburgh with Fife and the
north. The Victorian Rail
Bridge, **below**, was opened in
1890.

Left Until 1964 a ferry plied
to and fro across the Forth to
transport cars and pedestrians.
Now the elegant Road Bridge
spans the estuary.

Culross dates largely from the 16th century; preserved almost intact, it is now owned by the National Trust for Scotland. The Study (**above**) is a 16th century building; its nickname comes from the little room at the top of the tower.

Left One of the rooms in the Study, with a fine painted ceiling, a reconstruction of what it might have looked like in the 17th century.

Round the coast of Fife lie many picturesque fishing villages. Crail (**right**) is perhaps the prettiest of them all, with crow-stepped gables and pantiled roofs in a pleasing jumble.

Below Falkland Palace dates back to the 15th century, and was much favoured by Scottish kings as a place of retreat and relaxation.

St Andrews, **below**, was the first of Scotland's University towns—the University was founded in 1412, and still students may be seen around the town in their colourful red gowns. The town was created a royal burgh in 1140, and the cathedral was founded twenty years later.

But perhaps it is as the 'home of golf' that St Andrews is today best known. Here is the Royal and Ancient Golf Club, one of the oldest in the world. The Clubhouse (**left**) has seen the start, and the finish, of some of the world's greatest tournaments.

Opposite The Old Stirling Bridge, now closed to traffic, was built in 1415. Over these arches have walked every Scottish king from James I to Charles II.

The North East

Stirling Castle (**above**) perches high on a rocky hill above the flat carse lands of Stirling. Built at a key strategic position at the first fordable point of the Forth, the castle has witnessed many battles over the centuries.

Left The Wallace Monument towers high and cragged on the Abbey Craig, bearing witness to the loyalty and courage of the patriot, William Wallace, who began the fight against the English for Scottish independence.

The city of Dunblane looks towards its cathedral (**below**), a magnificent 13th century building set on the banks of the Allan Water. Below the cathedral a riverside walkway is named after a former dignitary, Bishop Leighton; 'Bishop's Walk'.

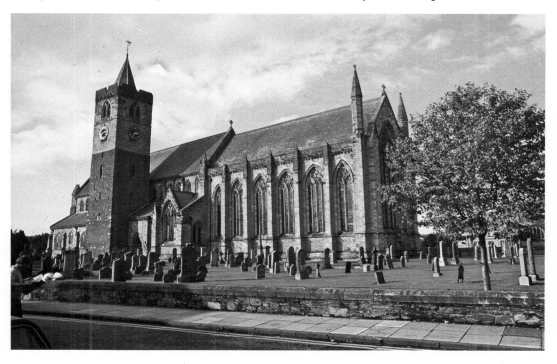

Doune Castle (**right**) is mediaeval, one of the finest mediaeval castles still standing in all Britain. Parts of the building date back to the 14th century. Many queens of Scotland have taken up residence in this once important fortress.

The village of St Fillans
(**above**) is at the eastern end
of Loch Earn; a pretty village
spread out along the lochside,
and a major attraction for
sightseers and for sailors, for
Loch Earn is one of Scotland's
premier water sport centres.
Right Another view of the
loch.

Top The Falls of Dochart at Killin. These ferociously tumbling falls are one of Scotland's most renowned beauty spots. The waters flow fast and free beneath the five-arched bridge, past the burial ground of the Clan MacNab.

Centre Kenmore lies at the eastern end of Loch Tay; a planned estate village in the precincts of the privately-owned Taymouth Castle, the whitewashed cottages stand neat and charming.

Right The Wade Bridge and Black Watch Monument, Aberfeldy. General Wade built an extensive network of roads and bridges for the Government in 1773, to aid military control of Scotland. The bridge at Aberfeldy was so sound that no alterations have been necessary even for modern traffic. The Black Watch, mustered here in 1739, was raised to control unruly Highlanders.

Castle Menzies (**left**), once the seat of the chief of Clan Menzies, dates from the 16th century. It was bought by the Clan Menzies Society in 1958 and restored. Today it is a clan centre.

Below Near Pitlochry is the new Loch Faskally, created by the effects of hydro-electric schemes in the neighbourhood. From a special Salmon Observation Chamber at the dam, visitors can watch the leaping salmon climb the 900-foot ladder on their journey up-river to their spawning grounds.

Blair Castle, seat of the Earls of Atholl (**right**). The earliest parts of the castle date from the 13th century, but many additions have been made over the centuries. Blair Castle, open to the public, houses many fascinating treasures.

Left Between Aberfeldy and Glen Almond the road traverses a narrow glen, known as the 'Sma' Glen'. On the valley floor, far below the mountain tops, the River Almond winds its way. Whatever the time of year, the Sma' Glen never fails to impress.

Right The Hermitage, near Dunkeld, poises above a roaring waterfall. The folly, built in 1758, was a retreat for the 3rd Duke of Atholl; under the arched dome, the thundering of the waterfall increases greatly.

Below Dunkeld is one of Scotland's earliest religious settlements; the 'Keledi'— servants of God—had a fort here in the 6th century. Dunkeld Cathedral was largely built in the 15th century, although it was destroyed in the Reformation. A series of renovations, the most recent in 1908, have brought the cathdral to its present condition.

Above Perth Bridge and the North Inch. The broad River Tay flows through the city of Perth; by its side are the North and South Inches— land given to the city by a rich merchant in the 14th century.

Perth, one-time capital of Scotland, is still impressive although few buildings of any age survive. One relic is the 'Fair Maid's House', **left**, the home of Catherine Glover, the 'Fair Maid of Perth', immortalised by Sir Walter Scott in his novel of that name.

Right Dundee from Balgay Hill, with the Tay Bridge. A former bridge over the Tay collapsed on a tempestuous night in 1879; a train which was crossing the bridge at the time went down also, and many lives were lost. Today's bridge can be relied upon.

Below Glamis Castle, seat of the Earls of Strathmore. This splendid Scottish Baronial castle was the childhood home of Queen Elizabeth, the Queen Mother, and here Princess Margaret was born. Stories of a mysterious secret room remain just rumours.

Opposite Union Street, Aberdeen, the main thoroughfare of the city, and impressively long and straight, was opened in 1805, a major engineering feat. The city of Aberdeen, far from the industrial belt of Central Scotland, is nevertheless enjoying expansion and prosperity, the results of the North Sea oil industry. The city is certainly an ancient one, dating back, it is said, to the 6th century, when St Columba's missionary, St Machar, travelled here from Iona.

Left Peel Place, Montrose; one of the most attractive towns on this scenic eastern coastline.

Below Stonehaven harbour, seen from above. The history of the little town goes back a long way; a 16th century tolbooth stands on the quay, and was used at one time as the local prison.

King's College, Aberdeen (**above**) was founded in 1494, and the chapel completed in 1505. This is a part of Old Aberdeen. The modern city, built largely of local granite, was constructed in the 18th century.

Left The Auld Brig o'Balgownie. Byron mentions this 14th century bridge in *Don Juan*. It was built by one of Aberdeen's bishops, Bishop Cheyne.

The north east of Scotland is notable for its many castles; among the finest is Craigievar (**right**), now in the care of the National Trust for Scotland.

Built in the early 17th century for a local merchant, 'Danzig Willie', using Aberdeen granite, Craigievar has an elegance probably

unsurpassed anywhere in Scotland in this type of tower house. Clusters of turrets rise above the clean straight lines of the lower stories.

Eighty-five miles of turbulent water, amid splendid rolling hills make Deeside scenery pleasing enough even for queens. And indeed, it was at the heart of Deeside that Prince Albert bought for his beloved Queen Victoria the estate of Balmoral. The present Balmoral Castle (**foot**), home of Her Majesty the Queen, is largely the creation of Prince Albert himself; with the aid of a local architect, the Prince demolished the original castle and built the present one to his own specifications.

Right The Old Brig o' Dee has survived the notorious floods which have swept away other bridges, and spans the river at the heart of Royal Deeside.

Opposite The fine view from the Brig o' Dee.

Left Aviemore, on Speyside, has been developed as a major sporting centre; on the nearby Cairngorms, you may walk, climb or ski. **Below** In winter Loch Morlich reflects the beauty of the snow-covered Cairngorms; in summer, these waters become alive with canoeists and sailors.

Opposite Elgin Cathedral, once known as the 'Lantern of Moray'. The cathedral was built in the 13th century, but was sacked and burned by the notorious 'Wolf of Badenoch' who terrorised the neighbourhood a century later. The Reformation saw the final deterioration of the building; today the ruins stand elegant and dignified on their riverside site.

Opposite Fort Augustus, once called Kilcumin, was developed as a military control post after the Jacobite Rising of 1715, and developed fifteen years later by General Wade.

Left Cawdor Castle, near Nairn. Cawdor achieved fame by its role in Shakespeare's *Macbeth*; but the present castle is largely 17th century.

In 1746, on the desolate battlefield of Culloden, a desperate struggle between Jacobite and Hanoverian forces saw the annihilation of Bonnie Prince Charlie's army, and the end of his bid for a throne. Old Leanach Cottage (**below**), was at the centre of the battle.

Inverness is the capital of the Highlands. The town stands on an ancient site, but its turbulent history has resulted in the survival of few old buildings. The old Palace of Bishop Eden now forms part of the modern Eden Court Theatre complex (**top**).

Inverness is linked to the west coast of Scotland by a series of lochs and the Caledonian Canal; a major waterway which makes it unnecessary for small boats to round the north coast and the dangerous waters at Cape Wrath. **Centre**, Dochgarroch Lock, one of the many locks on the canal.

The waters of Loch Ness are vast; and present-day fame is almost entirely due to 'Nessie', the water creature that supposedly haunts the depths. Sightings of Nessie are most common around Urquhart Castle (**left**), whose site was originally chosen, no doubt, for its fine views out over the loch and the surrounding countryside. Only the ruins of this huge 16th century fortress remain.

Above Dornoch Cathedral was founded in 1224, and was built on the site of an even older religious settlement. In 1570 the cathedral was largely destroyed in a local feud, and was not re-roofed until 1616. Further restoration was undertaken in 1835-7, and in 1924.

The splendid Dunrobin (**right**), seat of the powerful Earls of Sutherland. A castle may well have stood here since the 13th century, but today's building dates largely from the 17th and 19th centuries. The fine formal gardens were influenced by those at Versailles.

John o' Groats, the most distant point by road from Land's End in Cornwall, lies between Duncansby Head (the most north-easterly point on the mainland) and Dunnet Head (the most northerly point). The coastline here is spectacular, rocky and cragged (**left**).

Below Kirkwall is Orkney's main town; as in all island towns, the harbour is a focal point. Kirkwall's pride, however, is St Magnus's Cathedral, founded in 1127 by Magnus's nephew to commemorate his death in a quarrel.

Opposite The little community at Walls, Shetland. The oil boom has brought work and prosperity to Shetland, but many of the island villages remain untouched by the bustle. Peace can still be found on this distant island.

Top The Viking influence is still strongly in evidence in Shetland; and the annual 'Up Helly Aa' festival recalls the days when Viking warriors held sway in these islands. A Viking longship is carried round by torchbearers, then burnt to symbolise the death of Winter.

Centre The Pictish Broch at Mousa. This peculiarly Scottish defensive building is found largely on the northern and western coasts. The broch at Mousa is the most complete still standing.

Left The Shetland town of Lerwick. The life of the sea has always predominated in Shetland, and the harbour at Lerwick is as busy as any in Scotland.

Opposite The waters of the great sea-loch, Loch Eriboll, stretch away to the north; fine country this for the fisherman or the walker.

The North West

Above The northern coastline of Scotland at Durness. The shore here is fine and varied, with rocky outcrops and sandy beaches. But even on fine days the haar can sweep in from the sea and the mist can shroud everything.

Left Oldshoremore Bay, near Kinlochbervie. The sandy beaches on the west coast of Scotland can stretch for miles, deserted and idyllic.

Above Ullapool, busy fishing port and tourist centre of the north west. Ullapool was founded in 1788 by the British Fisheries Society to exploit the shoals of herring that swept along Loch Broom.

Right Loch Broom at Ullapool.

From Ullapool ferries travel to the Outer Hebrides; **left,** a relic of a former day—a 'black house' on the island of Lewis. The walls of these houses were built from four to nine feet thick to withstand the force of the gales that sweep unbroken in from the Atlantic. The roof was set on the inner wall to prevent it from being lifted off by the winds.

Below The standing stones at Callanish, Lewis, the best example of an aligned stone circle in Britain; 48 of the original 75 stones are still erect.

Opposite The beaches on the western coast of the Long Isle have no peer. Here, the sands of Luskentyre on Harris sweep magnificently away, silvery and unpeopled. The sands are largely the result of the weathering effect of the Atlantic winds—those same winds that keep the beaches unused.

This page The sub-tropical gardens at Inverewe. In this magnificent but barren corner of Scotland, the sudden lushness and colour of these gardens never fail to surprise and please. The estate, bought by Osgood Mackenzie in 1865, was no different from the surrounding land. Only determination and perseverance enabled him to plant these splendid gardens. Trees were planted as windbreaks, and estate workers carried creels of subsoil to lay the foundation of the beds. It took more than sixty years for the gardens to flourish.

Opposite Multitudes of birds nest on and around the many lochs of North Uist; on North and South Uist, there is almost more water than land, so many are the lochs and inlets.

Top The sweeping golden sands at Gairloch are one of the attractions of this northern fishing port.

Centre Loch Maree and Slioch (3215 feet). One of the most beautiful of the northern lochs of Scotland, the shores of Loch Maree are fringed by pines and deciduous trees, part of the ancient Caledonian Forest.

Left Torridon; an area of great beauty and enormous geological interest. Two vast Nature Reserves testify to the area's importance.

Opposite The peaks of Ben na Caillich near Broadford, Isle of Skye.

The island of Skye is unquestionably one of the most beautiful of Scotland's many fine islands—and one of the most visited. The Cuillin hills are renowned not only for their beauty, but for the excellent climbing they offer. **Above**, summer clouds over Ben Scriol are reflected in the waters of the Sound of Sleat. **Left** One of the glorious sunsets for which the west of Scotland is famous; Broadford Bay.

Top Loch Ainort, Skye.

Centre The village of
Portree, where Bonnie Prince
Charlie said his farewells to
the faithful Flora MacDonald
in 1746.

Right Dunvegan Castle, seat
of the Clan MacLeod.
The castle dates from the 15th
century, although many
additions have since been
made.

Above The Five Sisters of Kintail rear up behind the water of Loch Duich.

Left Plockton lies on Loch Carron, one of the prettiest villages on the north west coast of Scotland. Yachts and dinghies of summer visitors are now more common in Plockton's little harbour than local fishing vessels.

Opposite Eilean Donan Castle stands in a splendid setting where three lochs meet—Loch Alsh, Loch Duich and Loch Long. It dates back to 1230 although most of the castle was destroyed in 1714. Careful renovation early this century has restored its former splendour.

Above The town of Mallaig, the most important herring and shellfish port in Britain. The quay provides endless interest for the visitor, as trawlers bring in their catches of prawns and lobsters, herring, monkfish or the recently developed blue whiting.

Right The Ardnamurchan peninsula is wild and varied; at Sanna Bay, stretches of sandy beach contrast starkly with jagged rocks.

Opposite The White Sands of Morar. These beautiful silvery silica sands prove a favourite for holidaymakers and artists alike. Inland stretches Loch Morar, the deepest of Scotland's lochs.

Two memorials to Scottish soldiers; **left**, the Commando memorial at Spean Bridge, north of Fort William, tribute to the men trained in the neighbourhood who died in World War II.

Below The monument erected in 1815 at Glenfinnan at the head of Loch Shiel to the men who died in the Jacobite Rising of 1745 in the service of Bonnie Prince Charlie.

Opposite The great mass of Ben Nevis dominates the landscape around Fort William. **Top**, the view from Corpach. **Below**, from Ben Nevis the highest mountain in Britain, the views over nearby peaks is spectacular.

Above The Corran Ferry
runs just north of Onich,
linking Lochaber to the
westerly outcrops of Ardgour,
Sunart, Morvern,
Ardnamurchan and Moidart.

Right Loch Leven and the
Pap of Glencoe; a gentle
introduction to the wilder
scenery of Glen Coe itself.

Opposite Tranquil
reflections in the waters of
Loch Linnhe.

Opposite Glen Coe runs from Loch Leven to Rannoch Moor. The glen is quite spectacular; and its bleak aspect seems remarkably well in keeping with its tragic history. For here in 1682 took place the notorious Massacre of Glen Coe, when hundreds of Macdonald clansmen were murdered by Campbell soldiers.

Above Connell Bridge, north of Oban. Below the bridge race the Falls of Lorn; because of the rocks here, the tide flowing into Loch Linnhe creates a cataract several feet high. At flood tide, the waters flow back into Loch Etive.

Left Dunollie Castle, north of Oban, stronghold of the MacDougalls of Lorn. Parts of the castle date back to the 12th century, and the walls are very thick—ten feet in places.

Below The town of Oban lies at the heart of Lorn, and is the focus for all activity on this stretch of coast. Fishing is still an important industry here, but tweed, glass, whisky and tourism are important to local prosperity also.

Above Tobermory, main town of the island of Mull. In 1588 a Spanish galleon was blown up, and sank in the harbour; little of its treasure has been recovered.

Left The island of Staffa with its distinctive basaltic columns which surround 'Fingal's Cave'. In 1829 the composer Mendelssohn visited the cave and was inspired to write his Hebridean Overture, 'Fingal's Cave'.

Above Iona Abbey.
In AD 563 Columba landed on Iona from Ireland to spread the Christian gospel. Here are buried forty-eight kings of Scotland.

Right The Pass of Brander between Loch Etive and Loch Awe. Here, in 1308, Robert Bruce was ambushed by a party of MacDougalls, but fought them off. Loch Awe now forms part of a massive hydro-electric scheme; and an excursion can be made by minibus into the heart of Ben Cruachan to watch the vast workings of the pumped storage station.

Above Inveraray Castle, seat of the Duke of Argyll, chief of Clan Campbell of Argyll. The Campbells have always been a clan of power and influence; in the Jacobite Risings of 1715 and 1745 they fought with the Government.

Above The quaintly-named Rest and be Thankful between Glen Croe and Glen Kinglas is 860 feet at its highest point.

Opposite The waters of Loch Lomond, the largest area of inland water in all Britain. Loch Lomond is one of the most famous of Scotland's lochs, and its pretty shores provide a haven for the citizens of Glasgow, eager to escape the hustle-bustle of city life.

The
South West

Left The Falls of Falloch near Ardlui at the northern end of Loch Lomond.

Below A view of Ben Lomond from Loch Ard near Aberfoyle.

Glasgow is Scotland's biggest city, with industries which have traditionally focussed on the River Clyde—shipping, trading, ship-building. The Victorian age of industrial expansion saw a rapid development of the city, and it is notable for its many fine Victorian buildings.

Above The University, Glasgow.

Right George Square, at the heart of the city. The statue is of Sir Walter Scott.

Left Glasgow Cathedral dates back to the 12th and 15th centuries.

Below The Glasgow subway recently underwent a facelift; here is one of the smart new trains.

Right Helensburgh, with its pleasant situation on the Clyde, is a popular town for commuters to Glasgow.

The Holy Loch from Hunter's Quay near Dunoon (**below**); there is an American polaris submarine base on Holy Loch.

Above The still waters of Loch Eck, in the Argyll Forest Park north of Dunoon.

Left The Younger Botanic Gardens form a most attractive part of the Argyll Forest Park.

Right Ardrishaig stands at the entrance to the Crinan Canal; the nine-mile canal was cut around 1801 so that small ships could reach the Atlantic without having to navigate the difficult waters round the Mull of Kintyre.

Below Lochgilphead stands at the northern end of Loch Gilp, an inlet of Loch Fyne.

Opposite Jura means 'deer island'; and there are indeed many deer on this small island. The three distinctive mountains called the 'Paps of Jura' rise at the southern end of the island, visible for many miles over land and sea.

Right The sun sets over the Paps of Jura.

Below Port Askaig on the island of Islay; an island of great scenic variety, Islay is famous for its distinctive malt whiskies.

Right Brodick Castle, Isle of Arran. The castle dates from the 14th century, but most of the present building was the work of Scots architect James Gillespie Graham in 1844. It is now owned by the National Trust for Scotland.

Below The peaks in the northern part of Arran are quite spectacular; this is the 'Peak of Death'. The views on clear days extend as far as Ireland and the Isle of Man to the south, the Hebrides and the Highland hills to the north.

Opposite Campbeltown is on the peninsula of Kintyre which projects south towards Ireland; only a narrow neck of land at Tarbert joins Kintyre to the mainland.

Top Rothesay Castle dates back to the 13th century; the great curtain walls are surrounded by a moat, inside is a great circular courtyard. Partially destroyed by Cromwell in 1659, the castle was repaired in the 19th century.

Centre Rothesay is the main town of Bute, and one of the most attractive of the Clyde resorts.

Left The model village of Kerrycroy on Kilchattan Bay, Bute.

Opposite The seaside town of Largs looks colourful and festive at night; Largs is an attractive holiday town with good yachting.

Left Millport stands on Millport Bay, Great Cumbrae. The fertile islands of Great Cumbrae and Little Cumbrae are popular holiday destinations in the Firth of Clyde.

Below The harbour at the busy town of Irvine.

Ayrshire is Burns Country; for in this corner of Scotland the great bard was born, lived, and wrote most of his fine verse. **Top,** the Tam o' Shanter Inn in Ayr, once a favourite haunt of the poet, is now a Burns Museum.

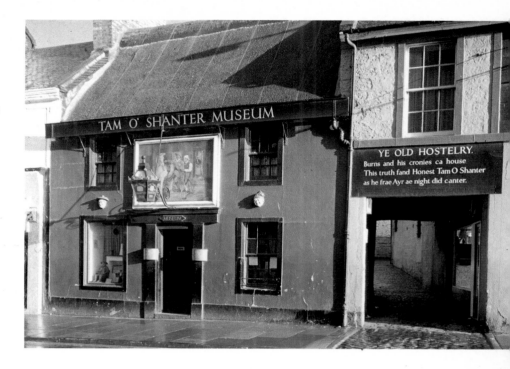

Centre Burns' Cottage in Alloway, birthplace of the poet in 1759. Thousands of visitors make their 'pilgrimage' here every year.

Right Souter Johnnie's Cottage is at Kirkoswald, a few miles south of Ayr. Souter (cobbler) Johnnie was Tam's 'ancient, drouthy crony' in the well-known poem 'Tam o' Shanter'. In the garden at the back of the cottage carved stone figures of Tam and Souter Johnny, with the innkeeper and his wife.

Above Culzean Castle, built
round an older building in the
18th century by Robert Adam
for the 10th Earl of Cassillis.

The castle is one of Adam's
masterpieces, and has many
fine features.

Right A peaceful scene on the river near the town of Girvan.

Below The island of Ailsa Craig, sometimes called 'Paddy's Milestone', as it is roughly half way between Glasgow and Belfast.

Left Wild goats in the Galloway Forest Park, a huge area controlled by the Forestry Commission and containing seven great forests.

Below This stone commemorates an early victory by Robert Bruce over a party of English soldiers at the start of his fight for Scotland's independence. It stands at the head of Loch Trool.

Above The ruins of Castle Kennedy near Stranraer, formerly a stronghold of the powerful Kennedy family. The gardens are splendid, with colourful rhododendrons and the first pinetum to be planted in Scotland.

Above Gatehouse of Fleet, the attractive little village that Scott called 'Kippletringan' in his novel *Guy Mannering*.

Right Kirkcudbright is the main town of the Stewartry of Kirkcudbright, the area that was put under the jurisdiction of the royal steward after the overthrow of the powerful Douglas family in the 15th century.

Opposite Threave Castle stands on a small island in the River Dee, with a fine commanding view over the flat surrounding lands. This was the stronghold of the Douglases until their estates were forfeited in 1455.

Above Dumfries, 'Queen of the South', stands on the River Nith. In the 12th century Lady Devorgilla, wife of John de Baliol who founded Balliol College in Oxford, built this bridge over the river. After her husband's death, the Lady Devorgilla founded New Abbey, now known as Sweetheart Abbey, in his memory.

Right The anvil at Gretna, over which countless runaway couples from England were married.